Contents

All sorts of food

Food is what we eat.

It helps us to grow and be healthy.

4

Food gives our bodies energy to do things such as running and jumping.

There are lots of different kinds of food.

What's your favourite?

5

Growing food

This is my tomato plant.

When it gets bigger, tomatoes will grow on it.

Then I can eat them.

7

Shopping for food

I'm shopping for healthy food to eat.

What shall I choose?

Fruit and vegetables

We made fruit salad with lots of different kinds of fruit.

I like strawberries!

I like kiwi best.

Fruit and vegetables are good for our bodies.

Sandwiches

I made it myself!

My sandwich has two slices of bread with jam in the middle.

Can you make
a funny sandwich?

15

Pasta

I used dried pasta to make pictures. See the different shapes?

Cooked pasta
is yummy to eat!

17

Treats

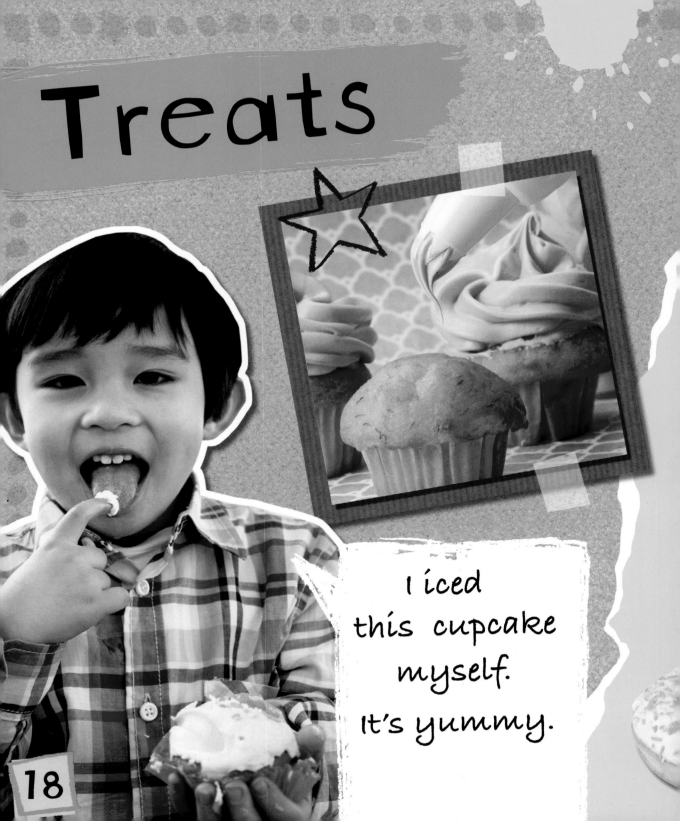

I iced
this cupcake
myself.
It's yummy.

But too many cakes and other treats aren't good for me.

19

Mealtimes

I eat three meals a day –

 breakfast,

lunch and tea.

Come on, teddies, it's time for tea. Let's eat!

With your friends

Café for Kids

Have a café with your friends!
First choose what food you want to
serve and make some menus for the tables.
Choose foods that aren't too hard to
make, such as sandwiches with different
fillings, carrot and cucumber sticks with
a houmous dip, fruit and a small treat for
pudding. Some friends will take the orders
and serve the food, and the rest will be the
customers. Then swap roles so everyone
gets to serve and everyone gets to eat!

Warning: Ask adults to check for food allergies!

Word bank

apple

bananas

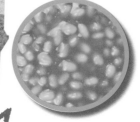

beans

bread

broccoli

carrots

cheese

eggs

kiwi fruit

milk

orange

pasta

strawberry

tomatoes

Index

Notes for parents and teachers

Growing food – Help the children to plant a tomato seedling in a pot with soil. Discuss how the plant needs sunlight and water. Encourage the children to notice how the plant grows over time, especially when the tomatoes start growing! When the tomatoes are fully ripe, let the children pick and eat them.

Shopping for food – Let children do their own grocery shopping. Set up a little shop with a variety of real foods. Discuss which foods are healthy and which foods are not. Then give the children a basket or trolley and let them make their own choices. You can even use play money and a till so they can pay for their groceries.

Fruit and vegetables – Make a fruit salad. Prepare a variety of fruits in advance, each in a separate bowl, for example, one bowl of chopped apples, another of sliced bananas, etc. Give each child a cup and a spoon. Encourage them to taste each fruit before choosing which ones they want in their fruit salad. They might discover new fruits to enjoy!

Bread – Baking bread is a fun learning activity. Help the children to measure out the ingredients and mix them together. They'll especially enjoy kneading the dough. When you put the dough in the oven, ask the children to predict what will happen.

Sandwiches – Help children to make their own sandwiches. Provide slices of bread; margarine or other sandwich spread; and fillings such as cheese, houmous, jam or mashed avocado. They could try making sandwich pictures, such as the one on page 15.

Pasta – Have the children make pasta pictures by gluing raw pasta shapes onto a piece of card. Point out that raw pasta is hard and not good to eat, but it's soft and yummy once it's cooked. Ask the children about their favourite pasta sauces and discuss how noodles are popular in many different countries, such as Italy and China.

Treats – Help the children to make easy icing by mixing together butter and icing sugar. Have them ice some cupcakes, but only allow them to eat one. Tell the children that the cupcake is a treat and ask them what happens if you eat too many treats. Discuss the difference between food that is healthy and food that is not.

Mealtime – Have a Teddy Bears' Teatime, either with real food or play food. The children will enjoy pretending to be the grown-ups, while the teddies are the children. Encourage them to talk to the teddies about the meal. They might try to persuade the teddies to taste new foods or tell them to eat up their vegetables, but not to eat too much cake.

⚠ **Be careful of food allergies when doing these activities.**